THE GOSPEL

THE POWER OF GOD FOR SALVATION

Matthew T. Beckish

The Gospel: The Power of God for Salvation

Contents

1. Important Questions

23 For the wages of sin is death, but the free gift of
God is eternal life in Christ Jesus our Lord.
Romans 6:23

The purpose of this short Bible study is to examine the Christian message of the great salvation that is found in Jesus Christ. What is salvation you ask? Salvation is God's plan to save people like you and me from sin and death. It is His plan to reconcile us to Himself so that, instead of death, we might have eternal life and be with Him forever. But why, you ask? Why would I need to be reconciled to God? I'm a good person, you say. Am I not on good terms with God? Listen, the Bible says that disobeying God's moral law, summarized in the Ten Commandments, is sin and that every one of

> **Salvation**
>
> God's deliverance of man from sin and its consequences.

- 1 -

us is guilty of sinning against God. The Bible also says that your sin has dire consequences. Your sin forever separates you from a majestically holy and indescribably righteous God who has promised to bring every single sin under His righteous judgment. The end of sin is death.

You see, your greatest need is to be delivered from the great calamity of your sin, and that calamity is death. The Bible says that, "the wages of sin is death, but the free gift of God is eternal life in Christ Jesus our Lord." Death is the terrible consequence for all who sin. Death is the consequence for the greatest of sins and death is the consequence for the least of sins. But there is a gift to be had from God, and that gift is eternal life. Through your sin you have earned death, but through God's grace comes the gift of eternal life. And this gift is offered through Jesus Christ – you can only be reconciled to God through Jesus Christ. Read what Jesus Christ said:

John 14:6
6 Jesus said to him, "I am the way, and the truth, and the life. No one comes to the Father except through me."

The Gospel

No one can come to the Father, to eternal life in heaven, except through the Lord Jesus Christ. To be without Jesus Christ is to be without the way of salvation. To be without Jesus Christ is to be without truth. To be without Jesus Christ is to be without eternal life. Apart from Jesus Christ there is only

> ### The Gospel
> An announcement of the good news of Jesus Christ, and what He has done to save lost sinners.

condemnation and the fearful expectation of God's righteous judgment for your sin. But through the Lord Jesus Christ you can have vast riches – the forgiveness of your sins and the promise of eternal life. To have Jesus Christ is to have sin and death utterly conquered. To have Jesus Christ is to have eternal life!

Friend, there is nothing more valuable in this world, nothing more precious, nothing more needful, than to be reconciled to God. There is no message in this world that is more critical than the good news, the gospel, of Jesus Christ! Let us, then, earnestly seek to understand this great message, for what questions could be more important than these: Am I right with God? How can I receive this gift and be saved from the consequences of my sins? The answers to these questions have eternal consequences. The answers to these questions are truly a matter of life and death.

2. Knowing God

23 Thus says the Lord: "Let not the wise man boast in his wisdom, let not the mighty man boast in his might, let not the rich man boast in his riches, 24 but let him who boasts boast in this, that he understands and knows me, that I am the Lord who practices steadfast love, justice, and righteousness in the earth. For in these things I delight, declares the Lord."
Jeremiah 9:23-24

So, let's get right down to it. What is the message of the gospel? Well, to start with, to begin to grasp the good news of Jesus Christ, we first need to begin to understand and know God. We can't truly understand the good news of Jesus Christ, or our desperate need for a Savior, without first knowing the majestically righteous and pure God of the Bible. Knowing God is the foundation of the gospel. So, with this idea in mind, let's take some time to examine what the Bible has to say about God. Consider the above Bible passage as you answer the following questions:

Based on the above passage from the Old Testament book of Jeremiah, when you feel the urge to boast, what should you boast in?

_____

What three qualities about God are listed in verse 24 of this passage?

_____

This is our mandate from God, to "understand and know" Him. So what is God like? Most people, when asked to describe God, will say that God is love, and this is certainly true, but the God of the Bible is not only love. According to our passage, God has revealed Himself to be a God of love, justice, and righteousness. Love, justice, and righteousness are the qualities God delights in, these are the qualities He unerringly practices. He is a God of love, justice, and righteousness! Each of these qualities of God's character are utterly perfect, infinitely glorious,

The Gospel

perfectly intertwined, and He always acts according to them. This is the God we must all come to know and understand if we are to understand the gospel. So let's take the time, next, to consider each of these three aspects of His glorious character carefully.

God's Righteousness and Justice

Let's begin by focusing our attention on God's righteousness and justice. The below verse gives us a good starting point on these two attributes:

Job 37:23
23 *The Almighty—we cannot find him; he is great in power; justice and abundant righteousness he will not violate.*

What attributes of God, listed in this verse, will He never violate?

_____

God will never violate His justice or His righteousness – ever! To be righteous is to possess perfect moral purity,

Righteousness
The quality of *perfect* moral purity.

and to exercise justice is to use one's authority and power to uphold what is right. God is infinitely good and always does what is right and He is also infinitely just and is an upholder of what is right. He is opposed to all that is not good and pure! And what follows is that, as your Creator, He requires you to always do what is right and just, and to fail to do so is what the Bible calls sin. So the big question is this: Does a perfectly righteous and just God really care when you sin? The Bible clearly answers that question. The Bible teaches that God is opposed to all sin,

> Justice
> The use of authority and power to uphold what is right.

He hates all sin, and will judge every sin ever committed. See these truths from the Bible:

Proverbs 6:16-19

16 There are six things that the Lord hates, seven that are an abomination to him: 17 haughty eyes, a lying tongue, and hands that shed innocent blood, 18 a heart that devises wicked plans, feet that make haste to run to evil, 19 a false witness who breathes out lies, and one who sows discord among brothers.

The Gospel

Ecclesiastes 12:14

14 For God will bring every deed into judgment, with every secret thing, whether good or evil.

Did you know that God was capable of hate? Name some things that God hates, and calls abominations, from Proverbs 6:16-19.

_____

Based on Ecclesiastes 12:14, which of your deeds will Almighty God, the Sovereign Lord, not bring into judgment?

_____

Maybe someone reading this already feels the stinging wounds of his sin and already has a sense of the righteous judgment of God that is to come upon the world. To you I would say, do not despair. This is truly the first step you must take on your way to being made right with Almighty God. Continue with me over the next few pages as the case for God's righteous judgment is made. But to you who takes sin lightly, take heed, and know that sin and unrighteousness are abominations to the perfectly righteous and pure God of the Bible. He sees all sin that is ever committed, and because of His infinitely good nature, He hates it. Sin is an absolute abomination to God.

You may believe that there are little sins and big sins, and that you have never done anything really bad, but this is not the case. The God of the Bible even calls haughty, proud eyes an abomination! According to the Bible, there is no such thing as a small sin, a sin that will go unpunished, "for God will bring every deed into judgment, with every secret thing." God is infinitely good and righteous and as a result, He will judge all sin.

God is infinitely good and righteous and as a result, He will judge all sin.

Do you believe that God will judge the world? Do you believe that God will judge you? After all, the Bible declares that "God is love." (1 John 4:8) Can one who is love actually carry out judgment? There are many people who believe that, because God is love, He will never actually carry out His judgment. Eternal judgment in hell is not only unthinkable to them, but impossible in their minds for God to actually carry out. Because God is love, they mistakenly believe that He must be incapable of hating and judging evil. Please know that these views are completely inconsistent with God's character as He has revealed it in the Bible. God has carried out judgment many times in the past (the Bible is full of such examples), and He will carry out His final judgment on mankind:

2 Peter 2:4-6, 9
4 For if God did not spare angels when they sinned, but cast them into hell and committed them to chains of gloomy darkness to be kept until the judgment; 5 if he did not spare the ancient world, but preserved Noah, a herald of righteousness, with seven others, when he brought a flood upon the world of the ungodly; 6 if by turning the cities of Sodom and Gomorrah to ashes he condemned them to extinction, making them an example of what is going to happen to the ungodly...9 then the Lord knows how to...keep the unrighteous under punishment until the day of judgment...

The Bible not only says that God is love, but it also warns us that God is unsearchably righteous and just, and that He will judge the world. Carefully consider this next passage of Scripture as well:

Romans 2:4-5, 8

4 Or do you presume on the riches of his kindness and forbearance and patience, not knowing that God's kindness is meant to lead you to repentance? 5 But because of your hard and impenitent heart you are storing up wrath for yourself on the day of wrath when God's righteous judgment will be revealed...8 but for those who are self-seeking and do not obey the truth, but obey unrighteousness, there will be wrath and fury.

These verses plainly teach that God's terrible wrath is upon all unrepentant sinners and that a day of judgment and wrath will be revealed. Every person will give an account for their life and will receive what is due for their actions. Please do not misunderstand God's patience and kindness, believing the lie that judgment will not come. The Bible says that, "God's kindness is meant to lead you to repentance." So what are you doing with these two precious gifts from God – time and His kind patience? In His kind patience,

The Gospel

God has not judged you yet. He has given you this precious time that you might turn from your sins. The real question is this: Will you acknowledge your own sins before God and truly turn from them, or will you store up this kind of wrath and fury for the day of God's righteous judgment? Examine yourself carefully! The psalmist writes, "God is a righteous judge, and a God who feels indignation every day. If a man does not repent, God will whet his sword; he has bent and readied his bow." (Psalm 7:11-12)

At this point in our study, some may be protesting. They complain, "That is the view of God from the Old Testament. The God of the New Testament is a God of grace and mercy, not a God of judgment!" This one-sided view cannot be further from the truth. True, you and I change. We change daily, we change constantly – our bodies change, our plans change, our attitudes change, our knowledge changes. But not so with God. The God of the Bible is immutable, forever unchanging in His character, His knowledge, His Word, and His decrees. (Numbers 23:19) The God of the New Testament is the same unchanging and holy God of the Old Testament. To further illustrate this truth, look carefully at some of the following examples that compare the righteous judgment of God between the Old and New Testaments:

Old Testament	New Testament
Nahum 1:2 *2 The Lord is a jealous and avenging God; the Lord is avenging and wrathful; the Lord takes vengeance on his adversaries and keeps wrath for his enemies.*	**2 Thessalonians 1:7-9** *7 ...when the Lord Jesus is revealed from heaven with his mighty angels 8 in flaming fire, inflicting vengeance on those who do not know God and on those who do not obey the gospel of our Lord Jesus. 9 They will suffer the punishment of eternal destruction, away from the presence of the Lord and from the glory of his might...*

The righteous wrath of God, revealed against His enemies, is in view in both of these Old and New Testament passages. Note from the Old Testament, the striking description of God in judgment – He is a jealous and avenging God, avenging and wrathful. Now note the Lord Jesus from the New Testament passage. On Judgment Day, He will inflict the same vengeance and wrath upon those who do not know

The Gospel

God and obey His gospel. See the unbending severity displayed towards His enemies – their eternal destruction away from the presence of the Lord in hell. Now, consider the following:

Old Testament	New Testament
Ecclesiastes 12:14 *14 For God will bring every deed into judgment, with every secret thing, whether good or evil.*	**James 2:10** *10 For whoever keeps the whole law but fails in one point has become accountable for all of it.*

Old and New Testament alike declare that, on the day of judgment, every deed will be brought to light – not some but all! Can a sinner's good deeds somehow outweigh his evil deeds, allowing him entrance into heaven? By no means, for, "God will bring every deed into judgment" and, "whoever keeps the whole law but fails in one point has become accountable for all of it." He has become a law-breaker, guilty and punishable before a purely righteous and immovably just God. Finally, consider the punishment God has declared for all sin:

Old Testament	New Testament
Ezekiel 18:4 **4** ...*the soul who sins shall die.*	**Romans 6:23** **23** *For the wages of sin is death...*

Your Creator has declared a just wage for your sins. All souls belong to God, He created us and we are accountable to Him, and this is the wage for all sin – death. There is no distinction, no little or big sin. Old and New Testament unmistakably agree: "The soul who sins shall die," and, "the wages of sin is death."

Based on the above New Testament passage from 2 Thessalonians, describe the actions of the Lord Jesus on Judgment Day.

_____

In light of these comparisons of the Old and the New Testaments, do you see the consistency of God's unchanging character? Why do you think God has revealed these things in His Word?

_____

The Gospel

From the preceding passages, you can see that God does not change. He is forever holy, and He will never violate His justice or His abundant righteousness. Even now, His dreadful wrath is heaping up on the head of every single unrepentant sinner, held back only by His patience and mercy, but for every single person that time of grace will come to an end. The Bible says that, "it is appointed for man to die once, and after that comes judgment." (Hebrews 9:27) Every single unrepentant sinner is only one breath away from God's righteous judgment. You are only one breath away from God's righteous judgment. And in the fullness of time, there will certainly come a day when the Lord Jesus is revealed from heaven with His mighty angels, in flaming fire, and every deed will be brought to light!

These things are inevitable, because God has willed them to be so, and He, unlike you and I, does not change. But listen, God has not revealed these things to frighten you into submission. On the contrary, in His great mercy He has revealed these truths about His unchanging, holy nature that we might know the truth and repent from our rebellion against Him. It is God's will that we not be deceived by mere opinion, but instead that we know Him. Read the below verse from the book of Proverbs:

Proverbs 1:7
7 The fear of the Lord is the beginning of knowledge...

It is a right, reverent fear of God that truly leads to knowledge. This kind of reverent fear or awe, though, is only possible as we come to truly know the awesome God of the Bible. Understand that the Bible passages presented in this chapter are only a tiny sample of what God has revealed about His holy character and the righteous judgment that is to come. Please heed God's call to seek to know His infinite righteousness, to understand His mighty holiness and justice. God's righteous judgment against sin is not some kind of character flaw to be hidden, or minimized, or somehow overcome. It is precisely because of His pristine holiness that He possesses such blazing justice! As we begin to rightly understand and look upon God, we ought to experience a feeling somewhat similar to what a child experiences the first time they see the mighty crushing waves of the vast ocean. Because God's perfections are

The Gospel

so exceedingly magnificent, they should be utterly jaw dropping! It is this kind of awe and fear and reverence of God that is really the beginning of knowledge. I pray that you will remember God's invitation to know Him and that you will become firmly rooted in the knowledge of the holy God of the Bible. And now, let's take some time to look at the third of God's wonderful attributes from our chapter's theme passage – His steadfast love.

God's Love

Can a God who is perfectly righteous and just and holy, love the unrighteous and unjust and unholy? How can one, who infinitely hates sin, love sinners like you and me? We will explore these most important questions in a later section of our study regarding the immeasurable love God has poured out upon His people through the person and work of the Lord Jesus Christ. But for now, let's take an introductory look at God's love in the following verse:

Ezekiel 33:11
11 Say to them, As I live, declares the Lord God, I have no pleasure in the death of the

2. Knowing God

wicked, but that the wicked turn from his way and live; turn back...

From the above passage, do you think God takes pleasure in the destruction of sinners?

_____

God swears by His own name, the highest of all names, that He takes no pleasure in the ruin of sinners. He must remain righteous, it is His unchanging eternal nature, but His joy comes as sinners turn from their sins to Him. God actively and lovingly pursues sinners. God rejoices in saving lost sinners. It is for this purpose that we even have the Bible – that we might know God and repent from our sin and through His great plan of salvation be saved! Read the below

Repentance

Sincere regret or remorse towards sin; A change of direction or turning away from.

parable told by the Lord Jesus Christ and carefully note God's joy in saving lost sinners:

The Gospel

Luke 15:3-7

3 So he told them this parable: 4 "What man of you, having a hundred sheep, if he has lost one of them, does not leave the ninety-nine in the open country, and go after the one that is lost, until he finds it? 5 And when he has found it, he lays it on his shoulders, rejoicing. 6 And when he comes home, he calls together his friends and his neighbors, saying to them, 'Rejoice with me, for I have found my sheep that was lost.' 7 Just so, I tell you, there will be more joy in heaven over one sinner who repents than over ninety-nine righteous persons who need no repentance."

According to this passage, how will God respond over the sinner who repents?

_____

God is portrayed in this parable as one who diligently seeks to save lost sinners, and as one who takes great joy in saving people like you and me. "Rejoice with me, for I have found my sheep that was lost," declares God when one who was lost is found.

God rejoices in saving lost sinners! All of heaven erupts with joy when a single sinner turns from his rebellion against God! Listen, we are all rebellious sinners and apart from God's loving mercy we are desperately lost. But all who truly repent bring the Father joy and will find His rich, loving mercy. He delights to show mercy, He loves to show mercy, and through the Lord Jesus Christ, He can show you mercy! This is every single person's desperate need, this is your need and my need – the loving mercy of God.

Awake, awake! Beware, for the wages of sin is death, God graciously warns! Will you heed His call to repentance? Will you accept His invitation to know Him? Will you heed this loving and merciful call for repentance from a perfectly righteous and just God?

3. Knowing Yourself

10 None is righteous, no, not one...
Romans 3:10

What does mankind think of himself? That question is simple to answer. All that you need to do is take a look at the culture around you to see that man views himself as very good and only getting better all the time! Scientific advances, education, new technology, evolution – these things are all leading to an eventual utopia according to the view of man. Mankind believes himself to be morally good. He believes that, with a few exceptions, he is upright. He believes that his heart is good. "Follow your heart," he proudly proclaims! Perhaps you find yourself in agreement with these sentiments. Perhaps you think that your heart is good. There are many people who agree with this view of man. But what does God have to say on this matter? What does God think of man? God declares, regarding all of humanity and without exception, that, "None is righteousness, no, not one."

None is Righteous, No, Not One

Read what the following passages from the Bible have to say about the state of mankind:

Genesis 8:21
21...for the intention of man's heart is evil from his youth.

Jeremiah 17:9
9 The heart is deceitful above all things, and desperately sick; who can understand it?

Mark 7:21-23
21 For from within, out of the heart of man, come evil thoughts, sexual immorality, theft, murder, adultery 22 coveting, wickedness, deceit, sensuality, envy, slander, pride, foolishness. 23 All these evil things come from within, and they defile a person.

The Gospel

Romans 3:10-12

10...“None is righteous, no, not one; 11 no one understands; no one seeks for God. 12 All have turned aside; together they have become worthless; no one does good, not even one.”

Based on the above passages, is it wise to trust in the goodness of your own heart?

_____

According to the last passage above from the New Testament book of Romans, how many people does God consider good and righteous?

_____

God alone is righteous – you and I are not. The Bible passages above declare that no one is righteous or good, not a single person. We are born in sin and we practice sin – our hearts are inclined towards sin. Our hearts are little factories producing all types of evil. According to the Bible, no one even truly seeks for God. We seek gods of our own invention (e.g. money, work, success, fame, self), giving all of our

3. Knowing Yourself

devotion and love to these idols, not even desiring to know the true God of the Bible. Can you say that you are any different? Is God absolutely first in your life? Have you ever sought to truly know God? Have you ever even bothered to read His Book to see what He had to say to you? Listen, you are not alone. The Bible says that every person has gone astray, doing what is right in his own eyes rather than seeking God. We are all unrighteous. We may think that we are good when compared to others around us, but the Bible's testimony is that this is simply not the case! Based on God's standard of righteousness we have all fallen dreadfully short. We are sinners. Do you believe the Word of God, or do you still believe that you are good enough to stand before Almighty God in judgment?

Consider these things carefully, and now consider again what the Bible declares about God and His judgment against sin:

- God won't violate His justice or righteousness.
- He will bring every deed into judgment, with every secret thing.
- The wages of sin is death and that the soul who sins shall die.
- None is righteous, no, not one.

The Gospel

How will you stand before this God in judgment?

The Ten Commandments

Up to this point in this study, we have used the words "sin" and "sinner" several times. To sin is to break God's moral law, and He has said that He will bring every deed into judgment. This means that every single time you break one of God's commandments it is sin, and one day you will stand before God and have to answer for your every deed. So, let's get specific and personal now and see if you are in fact a sinner. Let's look at just a handful of God's moral commandments, commonly referred to as the Ten Commandments. Examine yourself carefully and be as bluntly honest as you can as you answer the questions in this section:

Exodus 20:7
7 "You shall not take the name of the Lord your God in vain, for the Lord will not hold him guiltless who takes his name in vain."

Have you ever used God's holy name in a vain or casual way? Have you ever broken a solemn oath made in God's name (like your marriage vow)? How many times have you used God's holy name as a lowly curse word? According to the above passage, will He hold you guiltless?

Exodus 20:13

13 "You shall not murder."

Matthew 5:21-22

21 "You have heard that it was said to those of old, 'You shall not murder; and whoever murders will be liable to judgment.' 22 But I [Jesus] say to you that everyone who is angry with his brother will be liable to judgment..."

Have you ever murdered someone? You may not have taken a person's life, but the Lord Jesus taught that to even hate someone is to murder them in your heart and will equally bring God's judgment. Have you ever carried around anger and unforgiveness for a person?

Exodus 20:14

14 "You shall not commit adultery."

Matthew 5:27-28

27 "You have heard that it was said, 'You shall not commit adultery.' 28 But I [Jesus] say to you that everyone who looks at a woman with lustful intent has already committed adultery with her in his heart."

Have you ever committed adultery, cheating on your spouse? The Lord Jesus taught that to even look on a woman (or a man) with lustful intent is to commit adultery with them in your heart. Think about the movies and television programming that you enjoy. Think about the things you view on your computer. How many countless times have you looked lustfully upon a person, committing adultery in your heart?

Exodus 20:15

15 "You shall not steal."

Have you ever stolen anything? How many times have you stolen time from your employer? How many times have you taken something small that did not belong to you? How many times have you taken the credit for something that was not your own?

Exodus 20:16
16 "You shall not bear false witness against your neighbor."

Revelation 21:8
8 But as for...all liars, their portion will be in the lake that burns with sulfur and fire, which is the second death.

To bear false witness is to lie, or to twist the truth in your favor. How many countless times in your life have you lied? What, according to Revelation 21:8, is the reward for all liars?

Matthew 22:37-40

37 And he [Jesus] said to him, "You shall love the Lord your God with all your heart and with all your soul and with all your mind. 38 This is the great and first commandment. 39 And a second is like it: You shall love your neighbor as yourself. 40 On these two commandments depend all the Law and the Prophets."

The Lord Jesus elevates the moral law to the highest level in this New Testament passage. Have you continually and perfectly loved the Lord with all of your heart, with all of your soul, and with all of your mind? Do you continually and habitually give God the appropriate praise and worship for all the blessings He gives you in your life, rather than stealing that honor for yourself? Have you perfectly, without fail, loved your neighbor as yourself?

Through the Law Comes Knowledge of Sin

Now pay close attention to this next passage of Scripture:

Romans 3:20
20 *For by works of the law no human being will be justified in his sight, since through the law comes knowledge of sin.*

According to the above passage, how many people will be justified, or declared righteous before God, by their own deeds?

_____

What does this passage say is the purpose of God's law?

_____

Not a single person is righteous according to God's holy standards! God gave the law to reveal to you that you are a guilty sinner. Don't compare yourself to the person next door, compare your life to God's holy and righteous law. If you have been completely honest with yourself over the last few pages, you would probably admit that, according to God's law, you are a blaspheming, murdering adulterer, and a thieving liar. Consider the things you practice openly. Consider the things you do behind drawn curtains. Consider the things you do when you think that no one else is around or looking. God does not neglect to see these things, for He, "will bring every deed into judgment, with every secret thing." (Ecclesiastes 12:14)

The law is like a mirror, you look into it, and see the dirt on your own face. Now, you can deceive yourself and refuse to pick up the mirror, but that does not change the fact that the dirt is there. Pick up the mirror and take a good look. You break these laws every day – you sin against God every day! Do you think you can earn God's approval through your attempts to keep the Ten Commandments? This is the same God who says, "whoever keeps the whole law but fails in one point has become accountable for all of it." (James 2:10) You have fallen woefully short of righteousness. God's unbending law is meant to display the glory of His perfect righteousness and to convict your heart, to show you the dirt on your own face. Please know that before God you are a sinner. Please know that your heart is not good before God.

The Wide Road

"So I'm a sinner," you say. "So what? Nobody is perfect!" you complain. "Everyone I know does the same things. We are nice, decent people. We can't all be on our way to hell, right?" Consider the following words from the Lord Jesus Christ and ask yourself if sin matters to God:

Matthew 7:13
13 "Enter by the narrow gate. For the gate is wide and the way is easy that leads to destruction, and those who enter by it are many."

Luke 13:5
5 "No, I tell you; but unless you repent, you will all likewise perish."

Jesus says that there are many traveling on a wide road, many unwilling to turn from their sins, many who deceive themselves and choose a wide road to destruction. It is a very wide road that allows a person to claim to know God, and yet to live their daily life as if God does not exist. It is a very wide road that allows a person to attend religious services in the morning only later to spend their evening entertaining themselves with television programming full of sex and lust, murder and violence. It is a very wide road that allows a person to believe that they can love God with all of their heart, soul, and mind, and yet never even seek to know Him and His commandments from His Word. It is a very wide road that allows a person to believe that they have loved their neighbor as themselves and yet believe that it is alright to hold grudges and unforgiveness.

How did you answer the questions in this section regarding God's law? Do you not freely practice sin right now? According to God's unyielding law, a person who hates and is unforgiving is a murderer at heart. A person who merely looks upon a man or woman lustfully outside of marriage is an adulterer. Listen, a person who steals is a thief and a person who lies is a liar. You, like every other human being, are a great sinner before a perfectly righteous God. Liar, adulterer, murder, thief, blasphemer...these are all words that rightly describe you! God sees your heart and it is full of black darkness. You are not fit for heaven. The Bible says, "Do not be deceived: neither the sexually immoral, nor idolaters, nor adulterers, nor men who practice homosexuality, nor thieves, nor the greedy, nor drunkards, nor revilers, nor swindlers will inherit the kingdom of God." (1 Corinthians 6:9-10) Do not be deceived, the wrath of a holy God abides on the heads of all unrepentant sinners. Without real repentance you are walking a tightrope, with each perilous step risking a fall, straight into eternity.

If you were to stand before this God right now, today, what would you say for yourself? How would a perfectly righteous and unspeakably holy God judge you, innocent or guilty, heaven or hell? Doesn't this concern you? Where is your mind running to right now? Are you relying on your religious activities? They won't save you. God says that all of your righteous deeds are like filthy rags. (Isaiah 64:6) Are you relying on your law-keeping? That will never save you, you have broken every one of God's laws countless times. You are a law-breaker, not a law-keeper. How about your good heart? It is utterly deceitful! Listen, if you are being really honest with yourself it may seem hopeless. But there is hope! If there is a wide road that leads to destruction, there

The Gospel

must also be a narrow road that leads to life – to heaven. If God is loving towards sinful mankind, then there must be a way to be saved from this impending and frightful judgment. And so there is!

The Narrow Road

The narrow road that leads to life begins with a single step – a step of acknowledgment before God that you are in fact a guilty sinner who has rebelled against Him, a step that acknowledges that you have fallen short and have nothing good in yourself to offer:

Isaiah 55:6-7
6 *"Seek the Lord while he may be found; call upon him while he is near; 7 let the wicked forsake his way, and the unrighteous man his thoughts; let him return to the Lord, that he may have compassion on him, and to our God, for he will abundantly pardon."*

Friend, you have absolutely no hope of being saved from the eternal consequences of your sin until you come to the heartfelt conviction that you have utterly failed, and can never live up to, our holy God's standard. Your self-confidence must be smashed if you are ever going to enter His kingdom. Seek the Lord while He may be found! Call upon Him while He is near! Forsake your sinful ways and your light thoughts about sin, and repent!

Listen, I'm not telling you these things because I think that I'm righteous. I'm warning you of these things because I, too, am a bankrupt sinner who has been found by the compassionate mercy of God. As a bankrupt sinner, you are now being called to turn from your current way of life. Can you say that you are willing to go from a former life that all men live, a life of disobedience, a life of self-righteousness and ignorance of God, to a whole new life – a life characterized by a heart broken by your own personal sin? If not, there is currently no hope for you. If you die in such an unrepentant state, the Bible says you will surely perish in your sins. (Luke 13:5) Remember, true repentance is not simply a matter of empty words. It consists of a true sorrow regarding sin, and a change of direction – a change of heart. If you would be

> *...you must change your mind about sin and you must change your mind about yourself...*

The Gospel

saved, you must change your mind about sin and you must change your mind about yourself. You must turn from your sin and your self-righteousness and, empty-handed and helpless, you must turn towards God's help. If you are willing to do so, then there is hope. There is a way of reconciliation with a holy God. God, in His gracious love, has provided a way for your sins to be pardoned – there is a Savior!

4. How Can I Be Saved?

46 Thus it is written, that the Christ should suffer, and on the third day rise from the dead, 47 and that repentance and forgiveness of sins should be proclaimed in his name.
Luke 24:46-47

Ever since the fall of our first parents (Adam and Eve) into sin and rebellion, a fall that would plunge all of mankind under God's righteous wrath and judgment, our merciful God has begun to reveal His great plan of salvation, His plan to save sinners like you and me from the consequences of our sin. (Genesis 3, Romans 5:18-19) Listen, you are a sinner by birth and you are a sinner by practice. You have rebelled against a holy God in your thoughts, with your words, and by your deeds. But God, in His wonderful, loving mercy has provided a way of salvation for sinners! You cannot save yourself, but God has provided a way for you. The

The Gospel

above passage says that God has sent a Savior. He has provided a wonderful Savior who has saved His people from the terrible consequences of their sins. This Savior is the Lord Jesus Christ, and it is by Him alone that you can be saved! Is this message of salvation for you? Do you need to be saved?

In His Own Words, Why Did Jesus Come?

Consider the following words spoken by the Lord Jesus Christ:

Luke 19:10
10 "...For the Son of Man came to seek and to save the lost."

Matthew 9:13
13 "...For I came not to call the righteous, but sinners."

According to His words, what did Jesus Christ come to do? Whom did He come to save?

_____

4. How Can I Be Saved?

Jesus Christ came to seek and to save the lost. He came to save unrighteous sinners, separated from God by their sins. Friend, if you can't say to yourself that you are a desperate sinner, then Jesus Christ is not for you. He came to save sinners from the penalty of their sins. He came to save lost souls from eternal destruction. His call is not for the righteous, the one who mistakenly trusts in himself and his own goodness, no, the command of the Lord Jesus is one of repentance – a call to the meek and humble of heart, a call to the lowly, a call to the heart broken by sin. (Luke 13:5, Matthew 5:3-5) Do you hear His call? If you believe that you are good and not a lost sinner, then why in the world would you need such a Savior? The Bible says of you that, "the word of the cross is folly to those who are perishing." (1 Corinthians 1:18) However, if you can say in your heart that you are a law-breaker and a lost sinner in desperate need of a Savior, then Jesus Christ is for you, for He came to, "seek and to save the lost." Let us consider this great Savior now.

The Person of Jesus Christ

Jesus of Nazareth was surely a historical person, born of woman – truly a man. He was born into this

The Gospel

world some two-thousand years ago. But the historical person, Jesus of Nazareth, is not just a man – He is the eternal Son of God. This means that He is Deity – He is Himself God. The Bible says:

John 1:1-3,14
1 In the beginning was the Word [Jesus], and the Word was with God, and the Word was God. 2 He was in the beginning with God. 3 All things were made through him, and without him was not any thing made that was made... 14 And the Word became flesh and dwelt among us, and we have seen his glory, glory as of the only Son from the Father, full of grace and truth.

Colossians 2:9
9 For in him [Jesus] the whole fullness of deity dwells bodily...

Read the above passages carefully. In your own words, what are these verses saying about Jesus Christ?

_____

4. How Can I Be Saved?

The Lord Jesus is truly God and truly man – God in the flesh. The Lord Jesus was, and always has been God. In the beginning, before creation and for all eternity, He was with God the Father and He was Himself God the Son. And according to the Father's merciful plan of redemption, the glorious eternal Son of God, being born of a virgin, stepped out of eternity and became a man. He assumed human nature without any change to His Deity – His divine nature veiled in flesh. The Bible says He was "with God" and He Himself "was God," that "the Word became flesh," and that, "in him the whole fullness of deity dwells bodily." Do you believe the Bible's witness that Jesus is God in the flesh? The Lord Jesus said, "Blessed are those who have not seen and yet have believed." (John 20:29)

The Bible also declares that Jesus committed no sin, none whatsoever. He kept God's law perfectly:

1 Peter 2:22
22 He [Jesus] committed no sin, neither was deceit found in his mouth.

In every way Jesus was perfect. He continually and perpetually did the will of God – loving God with all

His heart, mind, and soul! He never uttered a word of lie – every word from His mouth was just, right, and true. Our Redeemer lived a life that was perfectly holy and righteous, just as His Father in heaven is perfectly holy and righteous. Can you imagine such a perfect life? Consider your own life in comparison. Countless times you have done what God has forbidden you to do, and countless times you have failed to do what God has commanded you to do! You sin against God daily, regularly, habitually. The Lord Jesus never sinned once. Regarding mankind, the Bible says, "none is righteous, no, not one." Not a single human being lived a life such as this, no, not one! No one could live a life such as this except God Himself. As Jesus said, "No one is good except God alone." (Luke 18:19)

Oh sinner, can you see His beauty and excellence? This is the promised Savior, the Lord Jesus Christ. The Bible says that there is "no other name under heaven...by which we must be saved." (Acts 4:12) He is the magnificently Righteous One, He is the God-man, and He is the purely sinless and only Savior sent by God to accomplish the forgiveness of your sins. It is in His name alone that you can be saved. Let us

4. How Can I Be Saved?

consider now how this great plan of salvation was accomplished.

The Crucifixion and the Great Exchange

The Scriptures said that the majority of those who lived in Israel at the time of Jesus, because of their hard hearts, would not recognize Him. He was their Messiah and King and yet they did not recognize Him, nor did they understand the words of the prophets that so often spoke of Him. And these same men would fulfill the very words of the prophets that they did not understand by falsely condemning Jesus.

Though they found no guilt in Him, they demanded their Roman occupiers to crucify Him, and so He was put on trial. At His trial the Roman ruler Pilate said, "I did not find this man guilty of any of your charges against him." But the people still demanded, "Away with him, away with him, crucify him!" Then Pilate said to them, "Shall I crucify your King?" But in their unbelief and envy, rather than submitting to Jesus Christ as Lord, the Jewish chief priests answered, "We have no king but Caesar." And so, Pilate, seeing that a riot on the verge of breaking out, delivered Jesus over to them to be crucified. In this way Jesus of Nazareth, who had been

The Gospel

attested to all by God with mighty works and wonders and signs that God did through Him, was delivered up, to be crucified by the hands of lawless men. But what lawless men meant for evil, God meant for good! Read the following passages and consider carefully what Jesus Christ accomplished through this seemingly disastrous and unjust event – His death on a cross:

1 Peter 2:24

24 He himself [Jesus] bore our sins in his body on the tree, that we might die to sin and live to righteousness. By his wounds you have been healed.

Isaiah 53:5-6

5 But he was pierced for our transgressions; he was crushed for our iniquities; upon him was the chastisement that brought us peace, and with his wounds we are healed. 6 All we like sheep have gone astray; we have turned— every one—to his own way; and the Lord has laid on him the iniquity of us all.

Romans 5:9

9 *Since, therefore, we have now been justified by his blood, much more shall we be saved by him from the wrath of God.*

According to the first two passages above from 1 Peter and Isaiah, what did Jesus Christ bear on the cross for sinners?

_____

According to Romans 5:9, what justifies, or declares a man innocent before God? From what are His people saved?

_____

At His crucifixion, Jesus Christ was pierced through, His body cruelly beaten and scourged. But why, what good could come out of this brutal death? The greatest possible good came! The Bible says that Jesus Christ bore our sins in His body on the tree – the cross at Calvary. He was pierced, crushed, and put to death to bring us peace with God! (Romans 5:1) His death on the cross was not an unfortunate, unforeseen

The Gospel

accident. The Bible says that Jesus was delivered up, "according to the definite plan and foreknowledge of God." (Acts 2:23)

You see, in order to remain perfectly righteous and just, God has promised to judge all sin. God must punish all sin. But in His great mercy, God chose to punish the sins of those He would save on a substitute – on His own precious Son at the cross. How unthinkably vile sin must be to this holy God and what unsearchable love He must have for us, that He would ordain the death of His only precious Son in order to satisfy His immovable justice and save us! Do not underestimate the vile wickedness of sin! Do not underestimate the magnitude of this sacrifice! Jesus Christ, the Lord of glory, willingly came to earth to die on a cross and save

Redeem

To free from captivity by payment of a ransom.

His people from their sin. Jesus Christ said that He came to, "give his life as a ransom for many." (Matthew 20:28) The heinous guilt of our sins was transferred to the Sinless One, and because of our Sin Bearer's death at the cross, God's perfect justice has been served, "for the wages of sin is death," and Jesus died on that cross for our sins. Jesus bore the guilt and punishment for the sins of His people on the cross in order to redeem us and reconcile us to God, and on the third day He rose from the dead, proving that His sacrifice was acceptable to the Father, our terrible debt paid in full. Fellow sinner, due to Christ's atoning sacrifice at the cross, see how God now views those who are savingly united to Christ by faith:

Psalm 32:1-2
1 Blessed is the one whose transgression is forgiven, whose sin is covered. 2 Blessed is the man against whom the Lord counts no iniquity...

Colossians 2:13-14
13 And you, who were dead in your trespasses and the uncircumcision of your flesh, God made alive together with him, having forgiven us all our trespasses, 14 by canceling the record of debt that stood against us with its legal demands. This he set aside, nailing it to the cross.

The Gospel

Romans 8:1

1 There is therefore now no condemnation for those who are in Christ Jesus.

According to these passages, how much sin will be counted against those who are savingly united to Christ?

_____

"Blessed is the man against whom the Lord counts no iniquity." Christ's people are blessed, blessed because their transgressions are forgiven, blessed because the Lord will count "no iniquity" against them, blessed because their sins have been "covered," blessed because they have been reconciled to God! All of our sins have been forgiven, not some but all, their legal demands canceled. They have been forgiven by a righteous God, not casually forgotten, not postponed, but paid for in full through Christ's death – nailed to the cross. The Bible says, "by a single offering he [Christ] has perfected for all time those who are being sanctified," (Hebrews 10:14) and that He has, "put away sin by the sacrifice of Himself." (Hebrews 9:26) As His people remember Jesus Christ's broken body and shed blood at the cross, we remember God's promise that all of our transgression, the full and terrible record of debt against each of us, was nailed to that cross with our Lord – paid in full, their terrible stains forever washed away!

The Bible makes it clear that man needs the perfect righteousness of God to stand before Him on Judgment Day, a righteousness that we can never achieve! Well, here we see the glorious gospel's answer to man's hopeless predicament. Christ has borne the guilt and paid the price for the forgiveness of our sins on the cross. But much more than that, through His sinless life He graciously clothes His people with His own perfect righteousness, the righteousness we so desperately need to stand before God! Read the apostle Paul's words:

Philippians 3:8-9
8...I have suffered the loss of all things and count them as rubbish, in order that I may gain Christ 9 and be found in him, not having a righteousness of my own that comes from the law, but that which comes through faith in Christ, the righteousness from God that depends on faith...

The Gospel

Consider the above verses from the Bible. Can you see what is God's answer to man's desperate need for perfect righteousness?

_____

In the passage above, the apostle Paul says that he gladly counted all of his achievements and deeds as rubbish, as filthy garbage. The inadequate works he had once self-righteously relied on to be made right with God he now despised. The righteousness that Paul clings to is not a righteousness of his own, but one that comes through union with Christ, a "righteousness from God."

Friend, God's righteousness can't be earned, you can't attain it by your own goodness, you sin every day. You need this perfect righteousness so desperately if you are to enter God's kingdom, but you can't achieve it. But there is a righteousness that you can possess. Jesus Christ offers you His righteousness. It is a glorious righteousness that is being freely offered to you as a gift by God's grace. You who are naked, who possess no righteousness, can be clothed by the Righteous One. You can receive the righteousness, "which comes through faith in

Christ, the righteousness from God that depends on faith." (Philippians 3:9)

Can you see the over-arching theme from the passages in this chapter? A great exchange has taken place. The Righteous One, Jesus Christ, who lived a life of perfect obedience to God's law, was punished in the place of sinners, and in exchange, He is offering to sinners the gift of His own unblemished and perfect righteousness. The Bible says, "For our sake he [God] made him [Jesus] to be sin who knew no sin, so that in him we might become the righteousness of God." (2 Corinthians 5:21)

This great exchange is being offered to you right now – your miserable sin and guilt in exchange for His glorious righteousness. Listen, apart from Christ you are bankrupt – all you have is your sin, unrighteousness, and the fearful expectation of judgment. But in Christ you can have vast riches – the forgiveness of your sins, Jesus Christ's perfect righteousness, and the promise of eternal life. Your salvation is not a matter of what you can do for God, but what He has done for you. Jesus did it all! Through His perfect life of obedience and through His death and resurrection, Jesus Christ has satisfied the demands of God's law and has saved His people from

The Gospel

their sins. And now this great victory over sin and death, bought by the infinitely precious shed blood of our Lord Jesus Christ, is being offered to you – you need only receive it!

The Free Gift of God

Friend, the only way that you can ever be reconciled to God is by His unmerited kindness towards you. You can't earn it. You don't deserve it. It is not owed to you at all. In fact, if salvation were based on merit, the exact opposite would be true. Before a holy God what you deserve is condemnation. But God, in His rich mercy, despite your life-long rebellion against Him, is offering His unmerited kindness and mercy towards you today. He is offering a gift to you. He is offering a full and complete and undeserved pardon to you. Read the following passages carefully to see how you can receive this great gift from God:

Romans 3:23-24

23 for all have sinned and fall short of the glory of God, 24 and are justified by his grace as a gift, through the redemption that is in Christ Jesus...

Ephesians 2:8-9

8 For by grace you have been saved through faith. And this is not your own doing; it is the gift of God, 9 not a result of works, so that no one may boast.

According to Romans 3:23-24, can you earn God's salvation through your own deeds?

_____

How, according to Ephesians 2:8-9, can you receive the gift of salvation?

_____

No man will stand before God on Judgment Day boasting of his good works and self-righteousness, laying out the list of accomplishments that have earned his entrance into heaven! Our best deeds are tainted by our sin and can only earn us condemnation before a perfectly just God. No, we are justified, or declared righteous in God's sight as a gift from God Himself, and not by our works. We need perfect righteousness to stand before God, but this righteousness cannot be earned or achieved. It is given as a gift, by God's grace, through faith in the person and work of Jesus Christ.

If you are in fact to enter heaven one day, it will not be of your own doing, you will have nothing to boast of, you have no merit. It will be by God's doing – by His loving grace. You will stand before God based on Jesus Christ's merit and you will be declared not guilty – innocent! And this amazing gift is to be received, not earned by your own good deeds, but received through faith:

Grace
The *unmerited* favor of God.

Romans 4:5
5 And to the one who does not work but believes in him who justifies the ungodly, his faith is counted as righteousness...

Romans 3:28
28 For we hold that one is justified by faith apart from works of the law.

4. How Can I Be Saved?

According to Romans 4:5 and Romans 3:28, by what means does God give His gift of righteousness to a man?

_____

These passages declare that we are justified, or given the gift of righteousness before God, through faith. Righteousness is counted by God to the one who believes in Jesus Christ for the forgiveness of his sins. The redeemed sinner does not trust in himself and his own goodness, but trusts in the One who, "justifies the ungodly!" The one who is saved by faith knows his sin, knows he is ungodly and undeserving, and by God's grace lets go of every shred of trust in himself and casts himself upon Jesus Christ alone. Look how these truths are further witnessed in the Bible:

John 6:40
40 "For this is the will of my Father, that everyone who looks on the Son and believes in him should have eternal life, and I will raise him up on the last day."

The Gospel

Acts 16:30-31

30 "Sirs, what must I do to be saved?"31 And they said, "Believe in the Lord Jesus, and you will be saved..."

The Lord says of the one who believes in Him, "I will raise him up on the last day." Do you believe this statement? Do you believe Jesus? Will you cling to these words and place your entire eternal destiny upon them? This is faith. To have faith has nothing to do with trusting in yourself and has everything to do with trusting in Jesus. To have faith in Jesus Christ is not simply believing facts about Him, but it means to trust your eternal destiny on Him and on what He accomplished at the cross. True saving faith says, "I am a guilty sinner, but Jesus died for me. And so, empty handed I come to thee." This, and this alone, is true saving faith.

Do you have this kind of faith? It is the only kind of faith that will save you. This kind of faith is a powerful gift from God and it has a powerful effect on every single believer! This kind of faith not only saves a person, but it transforms a person. This kind of faith will wash away everything that you once held dear and will radically change you. So I ask again, do you have this kind of faith? In light of the following powerful claims that the Word of God makes regarding the person possessing true saving faith, carefully examine yourself:

2 Corinthians 5:17
17 Therefore, if anyone is in Christ, he is a new creation. The old has passed away; behold, the new has come.

Ezekiel 36:25-27
25 I [God] will sprinkle clean water on you, and you shall be clean from all your uncleannesses, and from all your idols I will cleanse you. 26 And I will give you a new heart, and a new spirit I will put within you. And I will remove the heart of stone from your flesh and give you a heart of flesh. 27 And I will put my Spirit within you, and cause you to walk in my statutes and be careful to obey my rules.

1 John 3:9-10
9 No one born of God makes a practice of sinning, for God's seed abides in him, and he

cannot keep on sinning because he has been born of God. 10 By this it is evident who are the children of God, and who are the children of the devil: whoever does not practice righteousness is not of God...

According to the passages above, what is true of a person who is savingly united to Christ by faith?

_____

The passages above declare that the believer will be made a whole new person and, as a result, will live a whole new kind of life. God Himself removes the dead heart of stone from every redeemed sinner and gives them a new heart, God Himself puts His Spirit within them, and God Himself causes them to desire to walk in His statutes and be careful to obey His rules. The Bible says, "everyone who thus hopes in him [Christ] purifies himself as he [Christ] is pure." (1 John 3:3) The increasing desire for new obedience to Christ is the inescapable and inevitable result of salvation, a result of the new heart and the Spirit of God residing within the believer. For the first time in his life, the converted sinner, having received these precious gifts from God, will leave behind self-righteousness, and as a repentant sinner, will begin to engage in a life-long war against the remaining sin in his life, trusting fully in the grace of God to do so.

I ask again, do you have this kind of faith? Do you see your sins? Do you hate your sins? Have you turned in repentance from your old life of rebellion? Or are you happy to remain where you are? Are you happy practicing sin? Listen, if after hearing the gospel, you still believe that you are good rather than having a growing awareness of your unrighteousness before God, you haven't come to Christ, but you remain deceived. If you believe you belong to Jesus Christ, yet are pleased to remain dishonest in your business practices, you are a thief and you remain deceived. If, despite hearing the truth, it is your continued practice to entertain yourself with television programming full of sex and lust, you have no reason to hope that you are one of the redeemed people of God, but instead you are an adulterer and you remain deceived. If you claim to be a follower of Christ, yet are happy to habitually take the name of the Lord in vain, hold anger and grudges, and tell lies, you are not saved, but according the Word of God you are a blaspheming, murdering liar and you remain deceived. Please do not be deceived. The Lord said, "unless you repent you will all likewise perish." (Luke 13:5)

Without real repentance and firm faith in Jesus Christ, there has been no forgiveness of sins. Saved people possess a new heart given them by God and, as a result, are penitent people who hate their sins and by faith seek God's strength to turn from them. Saved people know they are sinners, trust fully in Christ's merit for their salvation, and out of gratitude and love for Jesus Christ, seek to live a life that brings honor and glory to God. If you have received a new heart from God, you will cease practicing sin and you will seek after Christ, following Him as Lord. You will still be prone to failure, doubts, and fears, you will at times be weak and fall into sin, but you will no longer be content to wallow in sin – your life will have taken a whole new direction. These are the marks of salvation, the sure testimony of God's merciful saving work, and where these marks are not present, there is no saving faith. Can you say in your heart that you are no longer the man or woman that you used to be?

Sinner, hear Jesus Christ's invitation. He says, "Come to me, all who labor and are heavy laden, and I will give you rest." (Matthew 11:28) Are you, for the first time in your life, feeling the heavy burden of your sin? Jesus Christ is offering rest to you, rest from the burden of your sins! Salvation is a gift, and it is being offered to you right now. This gift was bought at a very great price, it was bought with the precious shed blood of Jesus Christ, a sacrifice that is infinitely sufficient to pay for your sins and mine.

What kind of mercy is this? What kind of amazing grace is this? What amazing love Christ has shown to His people! "Come to me," He says. Come away from your sin, come away from

> *"Come to me all who labor and are heavy laden, and I will give you rest."*

your old life, and come by faith to the Savior. Jesus Christ is the same yesterday and today and forever, and He is more than willing and able to save you right now. He rejoices in saving lost sinners. But you must come by His way, through repentance and faith – there is no other way. The only remaining question is, are you one of His people? If you are, then listen to His voice and come – turn from your sins, call upon Jesus now, and ask for forgiveness. Commit yourself as a follower of the Lord Jesus Christ, the Son of God, and you will be saved.

The Gospel

Throughout this chapter, and this entire Bible study, we have attempted to delve into many of the truths of the gospel. Perhaps the Lord has illustrated the truth of these things best in this short parable:

Luke 18:9-14

9 He also told this parable to some who trusted in themselves that they were righteous, and treated others with contempt: 10 "Two men went up into the temple to pray, one a Pharisee and the other a tax collector. 11 The Pharisee, standing by himself, prayed thus: 'God, I thank you that I am not like other men, extortioners, unjust, adulterers, or even like this tax collector. 12 I fast twice a week; I give tithes of all that I get.' 13 But the tax collector, standing far off, would not even lift up his eyes to heaven, but beat his breast, saying, 'God, be merciful to me, a sinner!' 14 I tell you, this man went down to his house justified, rather than the other. For everyone who exalts himself will be humbled, but the one who humbles himself will be exalted."

4. How Can I Be Saved?

Unlike the doomed Pharisee who relied on his religious works and his moral achievements, the lowly tax collector, so convicted of his sin that he could not even raise his eyes to heaven, repented and trusted in the mercy of God. According to Jesus, this lowly tax collector went away immediately justified by God, while the outwardly religious Pharisee remained in his sin. Which of these two men are you more like? Will you, like this greatly mistaken Pharisee, stand before God one day listing all the great deeds you have done to earn heaven? Or, like this humbled tax collector, will you confess your helpless, sinful estate before God right now and seek His rich mercy before it is too late?

As a fellow sinner, a sinner who has been found by God's gracious mercy, I beg you to consider this message carefully. This is the good news of the gospel, the free gift of salvation through the glorious and majestic Savior of sinners – Jesus Christ. Now that you have heard the good news, has your heart been humbled in such a way that you cannot lift your eyes to heaven? Have you plead for Almighty God's gracious mercy? In whom have you put your trust?

5. Important Questions Revisited

17 So faith comes from hearing, and hearing through the word of Christ.

Romans 10:17

At the beginning of this Bible study we introduced a couple of important questions: How can you be saved from the consequences of your sin? How can you become right with a holy and righteous God? It's my sincere prayer that you now possess the answers to these questions. And so, before we end our study, I ask that you take a few minutes to write down the answers to the following important questions. Answer these questions based on what you believe in your heart to be true.

Who is Jesus Christ? Why did He come?

_____

5. Important Questions Revisited

When you die, will you go to heaven? What must a person do to go to heaven?

_____

The answers to these questions provide a good summary of this entire Bible study: In His merciful love, God has sent into the world His only Son, Jesus Christ, to redeem His people. Jesus Christ, the Son of God, came to seek and to save lost sinners like you and me. (Luke 19:10, Matthew 9:13) He lived a life of perfect righteousness in our place (Philippians 3:8-9), He bore our sins in His body on the cross (1 Peter 2:24), He received the just and righteous wrath of God in our place (Isaiah 53:4-6, Matthew 27:46), He died and He was raised from the dead, all so that sinners can be reconciled to a holy God. (Hebrews 10:11-14) Will you go to heaven some day? The Bible says that if you rely on your own paltry goodness and works, you will not. (Galatians 3:10-11, Luke 18:9-14) Christ alone is righteous, we are not, and His righteousness can only be received, not earned by your good deeds, but be received as a gift through faith. (Ephesians 2:8-9) The only question is, have you repented from your life of rebellion, sin, and self-righteousness, and wholly

The Gospel

put your trust in the Savior? If you don't, you will surely perish. (Luke 13:5, John 3:36) But if you have, if you have heard His call and trusted in the merit of Jesus Christ for the forgiveness of your sins, you will be saved. (Acts 16:30-31, Romans 4:5) It is the only way! (John 14:6)

Undoubtedly for some of you, your answers to the questions at the beginning of this chapter remain opposed to the glorious gospel of Jesus Christ. For this my heart breaks, and I urge you to repent right now, for the Bible says:

Hebrews 10:26-27
26 For if we go on sinning deliberately after receiving the knowledge of the truth, there no longer remains a sacrifice for sins, 27 but a fearful expectation of judgment, and a fury of fire that will consume the adversaries.

Hebrews 2:3
3...how shall we escape if we neglect such a great salvation?

If you find yourself in this position of rejecting God's truth, for whatever reason, I urge you one last time to consider your situation. You need every one of your innumerable sins atoned for. You need the perfect righteousness of Jesus Christ to stand before this God. Do you desire to die in your sins? If you do, then refuse to come to Jesus Christ, in true repentance and firm faith, for the forgiveness of your sins. If you desire to die in your sins, then trust in your own goodness. If you desire to die in your sins, then refuse His glorious gospel as presented in the Holy Scriptures, for the Lord Jesus Christ said, "unless you believe that I am he you will die in your sins." (John 8:24) Search the Scriptures yourself to see if the things written in this Bible study are true (Acts 17:11) before it is too late! If you find them to be so, then despising all pride within yourself, seek God's grace to humble yourself before Him and pray for His help that you might take these things to heart!

Moving Forward

And now, to you who has heard the truth and believed, to you who truly sees himself or herself as a bankrupt sinner in desperate need of a Savior, to you who has trusted in the atoning death of Jesus Christ for the forgiveness of your sins, to you who has repented and now follows the risen Jesus Christ as

The Gospel

Lord, I want to encourage you to believe the promises of God.

Know that our God has set His everlasting love upon you and that He will never leave you nor forsake you. And so, press on, trusting in the Lord. If you truly desire to be a disciple of the Lord Jesus Christ, you will not stop here. You must take action, but you must also count the cost. You must be willing to bear the scorn from an unbelieving world and follow hard after Christ. The Lord said, "Remember the word that I said to you, 'A servant is not greater than his master,' if they persecuted me they will also persecute you...In the world you will have tribulation. But take heart; I have overcome the world." Do not be surprised by the world's opposition when it comes. Don't be frightened by persecution. Keep moving forward with courage, trusting fully in the Lord Jesus and His promises. He will bring you safely through every trial. He is a great Savior, and He will never leave you nor forsake you. He has conquered!

Begin to read your Bible, begin to pray to the Lord, begin to serve others, and begin to be a bold witness in this world for Christ, proclaiming His gospel to lost

> *God will never leave you nor forsake you.*

sinners. Do these things every day. Be diligent! But please don't be mistaken, Christianity is not for "lone wolves." Join yourself to a Bible-believing, Bible-teaching church. Remember, no church is perfect (they are comprised of imperfect men and women), but join yourself to a church that believes Christ's gospel and teaches these things faithfully, for there is only one gospel and it is, "the power of God for salvation, to everyone who believes." (Romans 1:16) Know that we are called by the Lord to worship, to fellowship, to discipleship, and to service with other believers in His church.

Much like an infant, you have tasted the pure milk of the gospel, and now you must grow in spiritual maturity. From an infant, you must become like a young man or woman, strong in your knowledge of the Word of God. Eventually, you will become like a father or mother, mature in your intimate relationship with God, serving and encouraging other young believers. In this way, as a growing member of Christ's church, and by His loving grace, you will become a shining light in the darkness of this world, and your witness will bring glory to God.

May God bless you, and may you join in with the Scriptures in proclaiming:

The Gospel

Revelation 1:5-6

5...To him who loves us and has freed us from our sins by his blood 6 and made us a kingdom, priests to his God and Father, to him be glory and dominion forever and ever. Amen.

Notes:

Made in the USA
Coppell, TX
06 October 2020